# The Jigsaw Bible

I0171112

## Putting the Pieces Together

**Nathan Johnson**

ISBN: 978-1-78364-518-3

**www.obt.org.uk**

\*\*\*\*\*\*\*\*\*\*\*\*\*\*\*\*\*\*\*\*\*\*\*\*\*\*

**THE OPEN BIBLE TRUST**
**Fordland Mount, Upper Basildon,**
**Reading, RG8 8LU, UK.**

# The Jigsaw Bible:
## Putting the Pieces Together

## Contents

Page

*The Jigsaw Bible: Putting the Pieces Together*     4

# Introduction

# Introduction

Any student who approaches the Bible, the Word of God, must do so with some idea in mind of how to go about reading and interpreting it. Some have very little in the way of a formal systematic approach, and so approach the Bible more or less like they would approach any book, as something to read and understand according to their own thoughts and ideas defined by the culture in which they live and by their own personal experiences. Those who have more knowledge of the Bible and of the situations in which it was written, however, will apply this background knowledge to their reading of the Scriptures, and thus will come much closer, in many cases, to understanding what God meant by what was written.

Some will bring to their reading of the Bible many preconceived ideas taught to them by the church or denomination to which they have attached themselves. Others will come in with many personal ideas and thoughts about what is right, about what God should be like, and about how the world should work. All students, at some point, will come upon something in the Scriptures that contradicts thoughts already held, opinions already stated, or doctrines already believed. At times like these, one's faith is truly exercised. Which will win out, my beliefs, or what the Bible says? The answer to this question will determine whether the student will continue with unfounded beliefs, or will change them and so grow in knowledge, wisdom, and understanding of God's plan and purpose; past, present, and future.

The issue of right division is one of those issues which every honest student must face at some time or other because it directly impacts our knowledge, interpretation, and understanding of the Bible. This issue arises from 2 Timothy 2:15, which states:

> Do your best to present yourself to God as one approved, a workman who does not need to be ashamed and who correctly handles the word of truth.

The Greek word here for "correctly handles," *orthotomeo*, occurs only here in the New Testament. It is a word that was common among tentmakers, which we know from Acts 18:3 was the trade of Paul, the author of 2 Timothy. When making a tent, they would cut many pieces of cloth that had to fit together perfectly when the final tent was constructed. If these pieces of cloth were not cut correctly, they would not fit together and you would not get a tent as the final product. Thus, it was crucially important that you "rightly divided" or cut straight and along the proper lines the pieces of cloth if they were to fit together to make a good tent. Now this is the word that Paul used here for "correctly handling" the word of truth, the Bible. From the background of this word, we know that this must be an important task, and if we fail to rightly divide our overview of the Bible, it will not fit together into a proper structure, as it should. So the question then arises, "How do we rightly divide the Word of truth?"

# Types of Division

# Types of Division

The Bible is, of course, divided in many ways. It is divided into books, into chapters, and into verses. However, we must look deeper than this, to divisions in its theme, its message, and its focus.

The casual student, when thinking of thematic divisions in the Bible, will probably be able to list only one, which is the division between the Old and New Testaments. This division is clearly marked in all Bibles that contain both testaments, and so it is the most obvious. Most in Christendom seem to have the idea that the New Testament was written to Christians, and that the Old Testament is a poor cousin, which contains some good material for Sunday school lessons, but overall contains little for the believer today. I don't know how many would actually state it this way, but this is certainly the idea many seem to have regarding the Old Testament. We need to rethink such ideas, for all the Bible is God's Word and is useful in a variety of ways (2 Timothy 3:16); and, though it must be rightly divided, none of it can be dismissed as irrelevant today.

# New Testament Divisions

# New Testament Divisions

Now when it comes to dividing the New Testament, most who divide Scripture would acknowledge the division of the gospels, the Acts, the epistles, and the Revelation. However, few would admit that there is any thematic difference between these, or any real difference in their content or message. Most see the New Testament as one great whole, containing one consistent message, the only difference being the style of writing.

I think a thoughtful examination of the Bible will tell us a very different story. There are many things in even the New Testament that do not remain consistent from beginning to end. For example, consider the words of Christ to His disciples when He was sending them out in Luke 9:3.

> He told them: "Take nothing for the journey—no staff, no bag, no bread, no money, no extra tunic."

This seems plain enough, yet consider His words in the same book, Luke 22:35-36.

> Then Jesus asked them, "When I sent you without purse, bag or sandals, did you lack anything?" "Nothing," they answered.
> He said to them, "But now if you have a purse, take it, and also a bag; and if you don't have a sword, sell your cloak and buy one."

It is clear that Christ's commands to His disciples changed even from the beginning to the end of the book of Luke. Different circumstances changed His commands, and thus His message. Many of the so-called contradictions in the Bible can be traced to a similar change in circumstances, or to a revelation of new commands and plans of God.

Now, with this principle in mind, consider the difference between the following set of verses. First, consider Matthew 6:14-15.

> For if you forgive men when they sin against you, your heavenly Father will also forgive you. But if you do not forgive men their sins, your Father will not forgive your sins.

Now, consider Ephesians 4:32.

> Be kind and compassionate to one another, forgiving each other, just as in Christ God forgave you.

One of these passages suggests that we must forgive others, or the heavenly Father will not forgive us. The other suggests that we should forgive others because God has already forgiven us in Christ. These are two very different paradigms for forgiving. Which one of these is true for us today? For it is clear that both cannot be true at the same time. I believe that the Lord's statement in Matthew 6:14-15 was true for the Lord's disciples at the time the Lord told them this, but this later one, Ephesians 4:32, is true for us today. We forgive, not to be forgiven, but because God has already forgiven us. These sets of verses, considered together, show the need for some kind of division.

# Change brought by Christ

# Change brought by Christ

Among those who believe in right divisions in Scripture, one major division or turning point that is commonly acknowledged is the change brought about by the death, burial, resurrection, and ascension of Jesus Christ. Clearly, many things must have changed when Christ left the earth. During the period of history recorded by the gospels, Christ was walking the earth, ministering to men and dispensing the words of eternal life (John 6:68). When He accomplished His great work on the cross, however, many things changed. Our very faith and the gospel we believe, which is based on Christ's death, burial, and resurrection (I Corinthians 15:1-4) was not preached, and could not have been preached, before Christ had accomplished those things. In some ways, all of history could even be divided by that great event. Before Christ's death on the cross, sin and death reigned, the world was lost in sin, and every work of God with man appeared to fail. After the cross, sin and death are conquered, the sin of the world is to be removed, and God's work always succeeds in spite of the failures of men. So we can see that Christ's death changed many things. Thus it is not hard to understand that this was a great division.

What most who study the Bible do not understand, however, is that there is a second major turning point in the New Testament. A second great change exists, and it had nearly as profound an effect on the course of the New Testament, and the course of history, as did the death of Christ. That division took place later on in the history of the New Testament, near the very close of the book of Acts.

# Second Great New Testament Change

# Second Great New Testament Change

When Christ was about to leave His disciples and return to His Father, He gave them many instructions as to what they were to do and how they were to act. One of the most well-known of these, and in some ways the most controversial, is that set of instructions listed in Mark 16:15-18.

> He said to them, "Go into all the world and preach the good news to all creation. Whoever believes and is baptized will be saved, but whoever does not believe will be condemned. And these signs will accompany those who believe: In my name they will drive out demons; they will speak in new tongues; they will pick up snakes with their hands; and when they drink deadly poison, it will not hurt them at all; they will place their hands on sick people, and they will get well."

Christ gave His disciples their marching orders here. They were to go out into all the world. They were to preach the good news to all creation. Preaching everywhere was to be their part. God's part was to give signs to follow those who believed. They were to be able to cast out demons, speak with new languages, take up serpents, drink poison and not be hurt, and lay hands on the sick and have them recover. This would be how God would aid the gospel going out, and would clearly demonstrate that He was working with them.

Now many have noticed the odd circumstance that, though the gospel is still being preached all around the world today, God does not seem to be holding up His end of the bargain. That is, not all those who believe receive the signs that they should be receiving. Many find this difficult to justify. Some might blame it on us, saying that we don't have enough faith. Others blame it on God, saying He isn't true to His word. Others try to make the problem go away, citing some limited evidence that this passage was not in a few old manuscripts. Others try to deny today's reality, claiming that God is giving these signs to a few, to those who truly believe in them, and that these people have these signs. Yet there is a simple answer to this problem at the end of this very passage of Scripture, for in Mark 16:20, we read,

> Then the disciples went out and preached everywhere, and the Lord worked with them and confirmed His word by the signs that accompanied it.

It is here stated that *the disciples* actually did what the Lord commanded them to do. That is, they did go out, they did preach everywhere, and the signs did accompany them. We read about all of these things happening in the Acts of the Apostles. Some might find such a straightforward explanation hard to believe, since many teach that Mark 16:15-18 is our commission for today and that we are still working to fulfil it. But this commission was given to *the disciples* and it is stated clearly right here in this passage that *the disciples* already accomplished this. Moreover, it is likewise stated here that the Lord did His part. Indeed, we can see Him doing His part in the record of history given in the book of Acts and the letters written during that time. Notice that these things are stated in the past tense. They went out. They preached everywhere. These signs accompanied them. These things were done and completed. This is a fulfilled commission, and it was fulfilled before Mark ever even wrote his gospel!

# Mark's Commission Fulfilled

# Mark's Commission Fulfilled

Some may find it hard to accept this truth, but this is something that is repeated elsewhere in Scripture, and even more clearly. Let us look first of all at Colossians 1:6b.

> All over the world this gospel is bearing fruit and growing, just as it has been doing among you since the day you heard it and understood God's grace in all its truth.

Notice what is said in this passage about the gospel. Paul tells the Colossians *"All over the world* this gospel is bearing fruit and growing."* Mark's commission was to preach the good news to all creation. So if it had already gone "all over the world", could it be that this commission had been accomplished? In other words, had it already, past tense, gone out into all creation?

But we have one last verse that should settle the matter for us beyond doubt. That is Colossians 1:23b.

> This is the gospel that you heard and that has been proclaimed to every creature under heaven, and of which I, Paul, have become a servant.

The phrase "to every creature" in Colossians 1:23 is the same in Greek as "all creation" in Mark 16:15. It would be better translated "in every creation." It is a shame that the NIV has not translated this phrase the same in both passages, because they have translated away what, in Greek, is a clear statement of the fulfilment of what was said in Mark 16:15-18. Whatever Christ commanded His disciples in Mark 16:15, Colossians 1:23 tells us they accomplished it. The gospel has been preached to every creature, or to all creation, under heaven. This point, when the gospel had reached all creation, was a defining feature that marked the second great turning point in the New Testament. God accomplished His desire to have the gospel preached around the world. Now, He began a new objective, and started His people on a new mission. This was the second turning point in the New Testament Scriptures.

Now please note what I am *not* saying. I am *not* saying that we no longer need to preach the gospel. Nor am I saying that the world does not need to be reached for Christ. We need to do the work of an evangelist, just as Paul later exhorted Timothy to do (2 Timothy 4:5). Even from these verses in Colossians, it is clear that the gospel was still going out. However, what I am saying is that the disciples, with God working with them through supporting miracles, completed the charge they were given in Mark 16 and accomplished the commission they were to fulfill. The point when they did this marked a major milestone in the Word of God, and at that point a great change took place. God, having accomplished His purpose for His apostles, now began working towards a new purpose and goal. As students who seek to rightly divide God's word to show ourselves approved unto God, it is now our job to find out what this purpose and goal is.

# When was this change?

# When was this change?

When exactly did this great change take place? If you have followed along with me to this point, you will realize that we have narrowed it down to sometime between Mark 16:15 and the writing of Colossians, but we can narrow it down further than that. We can do so by defining certain things that were true while God was fulfilling the commission of Mark 16:15-18 through His apostles, and seeing when those things came to an end and were no longer happening. By doing this, we can find the point at which the big change most likely took place. We know that God continued to give accompanying miraculous signs right through the Acts period, the last ones being on Malta as recorded in Acts 28:1-9. And Colossians was written during Paul's two year stay in his own hired house as mentioned in Acts 28:30. Thus the point in time when God changed His purpose followed the last quotation of Isaiah's great prophecy (Acts 28:25-27). This was followed by the words:

> "Therefore I want you to know that God's salvation has been sent to the Gentiles, and they will listen!" (Acts 28:28)

When the Lord through Paul issued this statement that was when things changed. We don't have enough space in this study to consider all the implications of this verse, but we will focus on several important points. First, notice the word "sent." In Greek, this word is the verb form of the word "apostle." We don't have a verb form of this word in English, but if we were willing to coin a word, we could say that this verse declares that the gospel has been "apostled" to the Gentiles. What does it mean for something to be apostled?

Many define the word "apostle" as meaning a "sent one." While this is true, it does not set forth all the truth in this word. There are two Greek words for sent. One is *apostello*, the word we are considering, and it is related to the word for apostle. The other is *pempo* which is the simplest word for a sending, as *apostello* has a deeper and more technical meaning.

To illustrate these two different kinds of sendings, let us consider a family from the United States travelling abroad, say to Greenland. If a friend were to plan the trip for the family and pay their way, this friend would be sending the family to Greenland. This in Greek would be represented by the word *pempo*, for this friend was sending the family to Greenland. However, let us say that the President of the United States is sending this family to Greenland, and that he is doing this because he is making them the official United States ambassadors to Greenland. This is a very different thing from a friend sending a family to Greenland on vacation. In this case, they are being sent to Greenland with authority, and to carry out a commission on behalf of the United States of America. The Greeks would represent a sending in this manner, a sending with a commission and authority, by the word *apostello*.

Thus, Acts 28:28 is telling us that God's salvation, which I believe is embodied in the gospel, has been sent with authority to the Gentiles. Because the gospel is not a person, this word *apostello* has in it the idea of *authorization*. The gospel was authorized to the Gentiles. However, this word "Gentiles" is not an accurate translation. In Greek, this is the word *ethnos*, and it means "nations." The gospel of salvation was now authorized to the nations, meaning that all people from all nations on earth could now hear it and believe it.

Some might not see what the big deal about this is. Wasn't the gospel always available to all nations, they might say? Yet if we would really examine the New Testament, and particularly those books that were written during the period of history covered by the book of Acts, we would find that the answer to this question is *no, it wasn't.* Consider the words of Paul in Acts 13:26:

> "Brothers, children of Abraham, and you God-fearing Gentiles, it is to us that this message of salvation has been sent."

Here, "sent" is again a form of the Greek word *apostello*. This verse tells us that the word of salvation at the time Paul was speaking in Acts 13 was much more limited in scope. It was authorized only to the sons of the family of Abraham and the God-fearing Gentiles. The NIV is not very faithful to the Greek of this passage. A literal rendering of the Greek would read, "the ones among you fearing God." This does not refer to just any Gentiles, but only to those who were among the children of Abraham. These 'God-fearers' were Gentiles who believed in God and who attended the synagogues along with the Jews. Far from being authorized to all nations during the time period of which the book of Acts is the history, the salvation of God was authorized to the descendants of only one nation, the nation of Israel, and those Gentiles who were willing to align themselves with them and be "grafted into" the nation of Israel, as is set forth in Romans 11.

This is not the only thing that changed when the Holy Spirit through Paul announced that the salvation of God was authorized to the nations in Acts 28:28. Consider also the truth we read in Romans 10:12-15.

> For there is no distinction between Jew and Greek, for the same Lord over all is rich to all who call upon Him. For "whoever calls on the name of the LORD shall be saved." How, then, can they call on the one they have not believed in? And how can they believe in the one of whom they have not heard? And how can they hear without someone preaching to them? And how can they preach unless they are sent? As it is written, "How beautiful are the feet of those who bring good news!"

This passage sets up a series of things that were impossibilities when Paul wrote the book of Romans. First of all, it was impossible that those who called, whether Jews or Greeks, should call on One in Whom they had not believed. Of course, if they did not believe in Jesus Christ and expected to receive no salvation from Him, then they would not bother to call upon Him. Only one who believes has the right and the reason to call. And just as plainly, one who believes in Christ must first have heard about Him. They cannot believe in One of Whom they have not heard. And they can also not hear without someone preaching to them. In order for a thing to be heard, someone must proclaim it. All these things make sense to us, and are just as true today as they were then.

Yet consider the next impossibility that is listed in verse 15. "And how can they preach unless they are sent?" Here again the word "sent" is the Greek word *apostello*. This verse proclaims that no one can preach Christ unless he is commissioned and sent with the authority to do so.

This should seem very strange to us, because we know that we can preach the gospel to anyone at any time. No one has to send us to do it, and we do not have to wait for permission to do so. Yet this verse sets forth a very different picture. It declares it was an impossibility for anyone to preach without being sent with the authority to do so. This is not true today, but it was true when Paul was writing the book of Romans.

We might look at salvation in the book of Romans as being like an exclusive club. To join an exclusive club, one must first be invited, usually by someone who is already a member, and must be submitted as a member following certain rules. Joining an exclusive club is far different from joining a club with open enrolment, in which anyone who wants to join is able. In the same way, salvation during the Acts period (when Romans was written) was like an exclusive club. To be able to be counted as a believer, you had to be invited to believe, and this had to be done by one who had received the authority from God to invite you. No one could hear about the followers of Christ and simply decide to join. No one could simply pick up a Bible, read it, and decide to believe in Jesus Christ Who is proclaimed in its pages. No, to hear the message and believe it, one had to hear it from a proclaimer whom God Himself had sent. Only a God-commissioned individual could offer the message of salvation, and only through hearing the gospel from such a person could people believe. Those who were thus sent by God had His stamp of approval clearly placed upon their teaching through God working with them and providing miraculous signs to accompany the message. The reader should be diligent to search out the truth of this by examining these characteristics throughout the book of Acts.

This situation changed completely at Acts 28:28. Through the inspired words that Paul spoke here, the truth of Romans 10:15 was changed. Now, the salvation of God, the gospel itself rather than people, was sent or apostled. No more would people have to wait for a person specifically sent by God to speak the message before they could hear it and believe. Now, the gospel *itself* was the apostle, and it was sent to the nations. Thus, if the gospel itself was sent, it could no longer be said that only those who had been sent could preach, for now the ***message itself*** was freely authorized to all who would hear it. Since then anyone who hears it can receive it and believe it and preach it. Salvation is no longer like an exclusive club -- now, it is like an open enrolment. In fact, today people do not even need to hear the gospel preached, for simply reading it in the Bible and believing it would be enough. That is because salvation itself is sent to all nations, and the moment this started was when God moved Paul to speak his proclamation in Acts 28:28.

This point, Acts 28:28, is when the second great change in the New Testament took place. This is when the commission of Mark 16 was counted as fulfilled, and when God began to work on His newly proclaimed purpose and the next step of His plan. This was a major turning point in God's plan and work. It is a crucial and defining change, and we will never understand the Bible properly without understanding this transfer of apostleship from people to the message itself.

# What did it change?

# What did it change?

Now the next question we must ask is, if a great change took place at Acts 28:28 and the work God was doing in the Acts period came to an end then, what came next? What was the next great step in His work? What did He start doing that He had not been doing in the Acts period? Once we answer these questions, we will have started to define what is necessary for understanding what God's present work is, and what He is doing today. This is very important for any believer to understand. If we do not understand what God is doing, and what His present purpose is for this world, then how will we be able to act in accord with it, and live our lives in ways pleasing to God? Knowing what God is doing, and why He is doing it, is the only sure way to know how we can please Him with our lives and with the things we do.

It is now vitally important to realize which books of the Bible were written after the change set forth in Acts 28:28. Obtaining knowledge of when an epistle was written will help us to know whether its instructions were to men who were living during the Acts period, when the great commission was being fulfilled and a person could not preach the gospel unless he was sent, or whether it was written after that, when salvation itself had been apostled and when God had started His new work that He is still performing today. This is particularly important regarding the epistles, and not so important regarding history books like Acts. The book of Acts must have been written, or at least finished, after Acts 28:28, for verses 30-31 take us two years beyond that. But a history book like Acts receives its character from the time it records, and not from the time in which it was written. However, this is not the case with a letter and this is a crucial question for the epistles. Knowing when an epistle was written will aid us in understanding its message and its thrust.

My present understanding of the character of the epistles leads me to believe that the books of Paul divide up fairly evenly (or completely evenly, if one accepts the book of Hebrews as being written by Paul.) The books of Paul written during the Acts period, then, including Hebrews, are as follows:

1. Galatians
2. 1 Corinthians
3. 2 Corinthians
4. 1 Thessalonians
5. 2 Thessalonians
6. Romans
(7. Hebrews)

All these books were written during the period of time covered by the history recorded in the book of Acts of the Apostles. They all take their character from that time period, and reflect what God was doing at that time. This does not mean that they are not valuable, or that we cannot learn from them. As 2 Timothy 3:16 says, *"All Scripture is God-breathed and is useful for teaching, rebuking, correcting and training in righteousness."* These books, too, are profitable for these things. Yet, we must always keep in mind when they were written. They were not written directly to people living today. They were written to people living during the time period of the book of Acts, when God was working on a different plan and when many things were not as they are today.

The books of Paul that were written after the great change proclaimed by Acts 28:28 are also seven, and are as follows:

1. Philippians
2. Ephesians
3. Colossians
4. Philemon
5. Titus
6. 1 Timothy
7. 2 Timothy

These letters of Paul, written after Acts 28:28, reflect the changing character of what God was doing. Their message and focus are based around what God was doing after Acts 28 and so are most relevant for today: that is, the commands they give and the situations they describe match up much better with what is going on today than what we read in the Acts period letters of Paul. Because the book of Acts closes abruptly, without any statement about what God was going to do now that His work through the apostles of that period was completed, only in these last seven letters of Paul do we find stated what God's present work is, what He is accomplishing in this present age, and how we are to serve Him today.

Of these seven letters of Paul written after the change, one stands out as the most important in setting forth what God is doing today. This book, beyond all others, might be defined as the Book of God's Present Purpose. It tells us who and what we are in Christ, what God is working to accomplish, and how we are expected to participate. The book I am speaking of is the book of Ephesians.

# The Book of God's Present Purpose: Ephesians

# The Book of God's Present Purpose: Ephesians

Rather than go through the entire book of Ephesians, I would like to concentrate on what I consider to be the most important part of Ephesians for defining God's present activities and work, Ephesians 3:1-13. Examining this passage verse-by-verse, we can learn about God's activities today through Paul's inspired words.

**Ephesians 3:1.** *For this reason I, Paul, the prisoner of Christ Jesus for the sake of you Gentiles—*

Paul is continuing his discourse from chapter 2. He declares himself the prisoner of Christ Jesus. Notice this: he does not say he is Rome's prisoner, though he was brought to Rome as a prisoner under Roman escort, and certainly served time in his own hired house as Roman justice determined how to try him. Yet Paul considered his real captor to be Christ Jesus. Paul was where he was because the Lord wanted him there. If the Lord desired it, Paul could have been free and spreading the gospel as fervently as he had been throughout much of the Acts period; but now it was the Lord's will that Paul remain right where he was. So whether or not Rome was holding him was not really relevant in Paul's mind. He was where he was because he was the prisoner of Christ Jesus.

Then, Paul proclaims that he is a prisoner of Christ Jesus for the sake of us Gentiles. This is another change from earlier, when in

Acts 28:20, Paul declared, *"For this reason I have asked to see you and talk with you. It is because of the hope of Israel that I am bound with this chain."* That was Paul's attitude during the time of Acts. However, after Acts 28 he considered himself a prisoner on behalf of us Gentiles.

Notice that the New International Version has put a line dash after the word "Gentiles." I believe that is because Paul is now going to start what we could call a long parenthesis here. After starting this thought in verse 1, he is going to break off and go into a long discussion of something so important that he could not wait to bring it in until after he had finished this sentence he had begun. This parenthesis continues all the way down to verse 14, where Paul finally continues his original thought when he says, *"For this reason I kneel before the Father."* So what Paul started to say was to tell them about his giving of thanks. Yet now he has broken off, and in the next few verses he is going to share things with them of extraordinary importance.

**Ephesians 3:2.** ***Surely you have heard about the administration of God's grace that was given to me for you,***

Paul interrupts his sentence to insert this statement. It was his desire that they hear about the administration of God's grace. There is some doubt expressed here in the word "surely." There was a question: had they heard, or hadn't they? This question is still a good one to ask, for many around us still have not heard about this administration, or if they have heard, some may not fully understand it. Let us examine this phrase and its meaning very carefully, for God clearly wants us to hear about this very important truth.

The question is whether or not they had heard about the administration of God's grace. This is what has been traditionally called the "dispensation" of grace, for that was the way the King James Version translated this word. This idea of the dispensation or administration of grace is of central importance to the understanding of what is called "dispensational teaching." So what is this administration of grace? Before we can answer this question, we need to answer one even more fundamental, and that is, what is an administration, a dispensation? For we will never know what the administration of God's grace is if we do not know what an administration is in the first place.

In English, the word "administration" comes from our English word "administer," which means to deal out. Dictionary.com gives one definition of an administration as "the management of any office, business, or organization, direction." Basically, it has to do with the carrying out or enacting of a management. Yet if we want to truly understand this word in the Bible, I believe we need to go back and examine the Greek word from which this was translated.

In Greek, the word for "administration" is *oikonomia*. We can recognize in this word the origins of our English word "economy." This word comes from two nouns in Greek, *oikos* which means "house," and *nomos* which means "law." Put together we have *oikonomia* or "house-law."

I might illustrate this by saying that every time I enter a "house" for the first time, one of the first things I do is seek to learn its "law" about wearing shoes or not in the house. In some houses, the rule is that there will be no shoes worn in the house, and I would be in trouble if I tried to do so. In other houses, shoes are worn in the house, and the owners would almost be insulted if I did not keep them on. Of course, besides this there are many other laws in any house: who takes out the trash, who does the laundry, do you pray before meals, and so forth.

Therefore, from its basic Greek definition, an administration would be the way a person who is in charge of a house rules over that house. Yet as we examine this word in Scripture, we would find that this definition is too restrictive. We learn from studying the word "administrator" or "steward" that the word does not just apply to houses, but also to the managing of anything else. The word for "administrator" is *oikonomos*, and is closely related to *oikonomia*, as can be clearly seen. This word is used of household rulers, but it is used in a much different way in Romans 16:23b.

> Erastus, who is the city's director of public works, and our brother Quartus send you their greetings.

Here, the words "director of public works" in the New International Version are a translation of the single Greek word *oikonomos*. This man Erastus is called the "city's *oikonomos*." This clearly shows that the *oikonomos* was not just a house ruler, but could also be a ruler over a much larger group of people. Applying this lesson to the word *oikonomia*, we conclude that the word "administration" can be applied to rule over others in many different contexts, not just that of a household. To limit it to rule over one's own house does not fit with the facts presented in Scripture.

Thus, when we speak of an administration in the Bible, we are speaking of the way a group of people (such as a household, but not limited to a household,) are ruled or managed. When we speak of administrations, or dispensations, in a Biblical sense, although the word is not used exclusively for God's administrations in the pages of Scripture, we are usually talking about administrations of

God. These are *His policies towards the earth and the people living upon it,* and they have changed over time. God's current administration is His power enacted over the earth.

So we might define the dispensation or administration of God's grace as being God's policy of grace. There are many questions that people ask about God that can be answered by understanding that God's administration and His policy towards the earth today is one of grace. What will God do about the wicked things and wicked men of this world, one might ask? And we could answer, His policy is grace. That is He will not remove them with judgment, but will wait patiently, giving wicked men every opportunity to repent; i.e. He acts in grace. In anything and everything, God's activities regarding this earth are always and exclusively gracious. He always acts in grace, and when He cannot act in grace, He will not act at all.

God's policy has not always been gracious. Certainly, grace has always been an important part of His character and nature. Ever since He did not kill Adam and Eve immediately in the garden, He has shown His grace to those who did not deserve it. Yet in spite of the fact that God was very gracious in many dealings of the past, we could also point to many other times where God acted in judgment, setting things in order as He saw fit. God's grace gives favour to men who do not deserve it, but God's judgment gives men exactly what they deserve. For example, in the flood, God wiped out all life on the earth save what was in the Ark, which was a very judgmental act. God commanded the Israelites to wipe out the Canaanites when He sent them to inherit the land, which was a definite act of judgment by God upon the Canaanites. When God finally brought destruction upon Jerusalem for all their sins and unfaithfulness to Him, this was an act of judgment, and totally the opposite of grace. Yet God saved

Noah and his family in the Ark, which was a very gracious act. He delivered Israel from slavery and brought them to their promised land in spite of all their stubbornness and rebellion, which was also a very gracious act. He allowed a small remnant of Israelites to escape the destruction of Jerusalem by Nebuchadnezzar, and later brought them back to their land, which was certainly gracious and undeserved. In all these things, God acted toward some in judgment, and toward others in grace.

In the past, God has worked sometimes in grace, and sometimes in judgment and fairness. Yet in the administration of grace, God has limited Himself to only acting in grace. It is like He has tied the hand of judgment behind His back, and will only act with the hand of grace. Note that He has limited Himself. No one else could limit Him. He has tied His Own hand behind His back. No one else could tie His hands. When I declare that God will only act in grace today, never in judgment, some will accuse me of "limiting God." But that is not the case. God cannot be limited by men. He can only limit Himself and He has limited Himself. Anyone who looks at the world today must admit that He could do far more than He is doing for the world. Either this is all that God is capable of, or He is limiting Himself somehow. Ephesians 3:3 tells us what He is doing, how He is limiting Himself, and why. Some prefer to think, or at least imply, that God governs the world based on His whims of the moment. Yet if we study this passage, we find the truth. We know what God is doing today, namely acting exclusively in grace. That is the basis of God's present administration of grace. Furthermore, our knowing this is not restricting God, but is actually bringing glory to Him by our acknowledging and treasuring His present work.

This administration of God's grace was "given to me for you." This means that Paul was given the revelation of this administration of grace so that he could pass it on to his readers for our benefit. Let us read this section carefully so that we can benefit from what God is going to tell us through Paul about His current administration.

**Ephesians 3:3.** *that is, the mystery made known to me by revelation, as I have already written briefly.*

Both the administration of God's grace and the mystery were made known to Paul by revelation. The word translated "revelation" is the Greek word *apokalupsis*, and means an "unveiling." In this case, God unveiled to Paul the plan which He had formerly kept entirely secret. Now, God has made known to him this mystery.

What is a mystery? This question must be answered before we can say anything intelligent about what the "mystery" here might be. In Greek, the word is *musterion*. This word has been transliterated, not translated, into English. "U" and "y" are the same letter in Greek, and "ion" is just a Greek ending that we change to "y" to make "mystery." However, in English the word "mystery" means something unknown which men must puzzle over in an attempt to "solve" it. The Greek word *musterion*, however, meant more along the lines of our English word "secret." God particularly uses this word when speaking of something that was part of His plan but that He had previously left unrevealed. Now, however, He has broken His silence concerning it, and has set it forth for all who care to listen and understand. Thus, a "mystery" is a Divinely-held secret that has now been revealed.

Some have tried to expand this word "mystery" into a general label for all the teaching of this dispensation. They call all truth for today by the general label "mystery truth." Then, when they find the word "mystery" in Paul's earlier letters, in Romans 11:25, 16:25; I Corinthians 2:7, 4:1, 13:2, 14:2, 15:51; and 2 Thessalonians 2:7, they declare that this proves that the dispensation of grace had already begun with the call and commissioning of Paul, and that the latter half of the Acts period was a "transition period" into the dispensation of grace. Yet those who make this argument seem to ignore the fact that Christ used the word "mystery" as well; see Matthew 13:11, Mark 4:11, and Luke 8:10. If the mere presence of the word proves that the dispensational change had already taken place, then even Christ's ministry would have to be included in our current dispensation!

The fact is the word "mystery" is used whenever any revelation from God that had previously been hidden is set forth. There were such revelations in Christ's ministry, there were such revelations in Paul's ministry during the Acts period, there are such revelations in the later letters of Paul that were written for believers today, and there are even such revelations in the book of Revelation written about times yet future. The word "mystery" has no special meaning that makes it apply only to the truths of our dispensation today.

Though the Bible speaks of many mysteries or secrets, there is one great truth set forth in the books of Ephesians and Colossians that could be called "THE mystery" for today. This is the previously unrevealed secret of God's current management of His people – God's administration of grace - that Paul is about to set forth here in Ephesians 3. This is "THE" secret of God for us today. This is not the only mystery in Scripture, but it is the one that is most important to God's current plan and program for the world.

Paul now says that he had "already written briefly" of this secret. These words have puzzled many, and others have tried to find this brief writing to which Paul is referring. Some believe that they find it in the words of Paul in Romans 16:25-26, while others speculate about a "lost epistle" of Paul that contains this brief record. Yet I believe that these are looking in the wrong place, for Paul is not referring to some other writing of his, but rather to something he has written briefly about in this very letter that we are currently studying. His words here are similar to if I should refer to something earlier in this writing, and should say something like "see above" or "as I said previously."

Paul is most likely talking about his words in Ephesians 1:9, where he wrote of God, "*And he made known to us the mystery of his will according to his good pleasure, which he purposed in Christ.*" This was a brief reference to God's current work that has to do with the previously unrevealed secret of His will for the current dispensation. We will learn more about what this will is as we follow out this passage.

**Ephesians 3:4.** *In reading this, then, you will be able to understand my insight into the mystery of Christ,*

Paul does not mean he wants them to be impressed by realizing how much he knows. Rather, he is concerned that they gain knowledge. By getting to know this mystery, they will have the power to understand what Paul already knows regarding this mystery of Christ. We must seek to know before we can expect to understand.

**Ephesians 3:5.** *which was not made known to men in other generations as it has now been revealed by the Spirit to God's holy apostles and prophets.*

Paul states that God had never made known this mystery to men in any of his revelations prior to this time. It was a secret that He had hidden in Himself. This was true no longer. Now, He had revealed it by the Spirit to His holy apostles and prophets. This was a new revelation that no one had known before.

This new revelation of the truth of the secret had now been revealed to God's holy apostles and prophets. Many will ask, "Who these apostles and prophets were to whom God revealed the mystery?" For we understand that we live in a time when *"there is one God and one mediator between God and men, the man Christ Jesus,"* 1 Timothy 2:5. As such, God-commissioned apostles and prophets who can speak the words of God to others have no place in this dispensation. So who were the "apostles and prophets" to whom this revelation was made?

I would suggest that these were the very same local apostles and prophets that had been active among the believers in every city during the Acts period. Those people who believed during the Acts period would have been taken by surprise by this great, administrational change. No one was expecting it, for it was a secret hidden in God. Whom would they believe if God sent someone to tell them of this unexpected change? Who else but those whom they already knew were the prophets and apostles of God? Otherwise, we would have to imagine the calling of a whole new set of apostles and prophets, and this definitely does not seem to fit with the time in which we live.

It is important to recognize that there was a period between the great proclamation at Acts 28:28, when God's new dispensation had begun, and when Paul completed the Bible by writing 2 Timothy. During this period, His complete silence had not yet commenced. This was a time when God was revealing the truths for the current time and in a way "sweeping up" and bringing to a close that great work that He had done in the Acts period. He did not just drop all those believers like a hot potato. They deserved some sort of explanation from God as to what had happened, and they got it. This was through their own, local apostles and prophets that had served them in the Acts period, as well as through the Ephesian letter.

**Ephesians 3:6.** *This mystery is that through the gospel the* *Gentiles are heirs together with Israel, members together of one* *body, and sharers together in the promise in Christ Jesus.*

This is the heart of what the mystery is. We need some clarification as to the Greek words used here. First of all, the word for "Gentiles" is a plural form of *ethnos*, which simply means nations. To exclude Israel from these things, as if they applied to all other nations but theirs, is simply not true to what the Spirit is saying here. Secondly, there is a common prefix *sun* in Greek before the three words "heirs," "body," and "sharers." The NIV has represented this by the word "together." We might translate this prefix by something like "joint" or "equal." The emphasis is on complete equality here. All people of all nations, including Israel, who believe in Christ are equal heirs, equal sharers, and equal members. No one nation is now preferred above another.

Some have declared that the mystery merely means that Gentiles can be saved today, not just Israelites. Others suggest that the mystery means that all nations, not just Israel, can now receive blessings from God. Yet neither of these things was a secret. From ancient times God had given His promise that all nations of the earth would be blessed. God promised Abraham in Genesis 22:18, "and through your offspring all nations on earth will be blessed, because you have obeyed me." God's plan has always included blessings for all nations. What was new in this was not that other nations besides Israel would be blessed. Always in the Old Testament, the blessings that the nations would receive were pictured as flowing to them *through* Israel. Israel was to be the mediatorial nation to bring blessings to the rest of the world. The secret, which had never before been revealed, was that all nations would be blessed equally and jointly alongside of Israel. They were not to be subservient to Israel, but to be blessed right alongside them. This was a new truth that had never before been revealed. This was the truth of the secret that was being revealed here.

This truth was something new when Paul was writing Ephesians. This had not been true during the Old Testament and not during the Gospels either. And it was not true during the period of time covered by the Acts of the Apostles; e.g. see Romans 1:16; 2:9-10. We can also clearly see this in Romans 11:11-24, where the Gentiles are set forth as a wild olive branch grafted into the good olive tree of Israel, partaking of their nourishing sap. The entire passage should be read in this context, but verse 18 is a good summary of its teaching on the position of the Gentiles at that time.

> Do not boast over those branches. If you do, consider this: You do not support the root, but the root supports you.

The Gentile believers of the Acts period were grafted into Israel, and were supported by Israel. They were in no way joint or equal with them. The truth of Ephesians 3:6 was not true then. In fact, Romans 11:18 and Ephesians 3:6 are mutually exclusive. One cannot be true as long as the other is true. The Gentiles can either be dependent branches grafted into Israel, or they can be equal and joint with Israel. Therefore, we can see that in this regard the administrational change at Acts 28:28 is critical to a correct understanding of these two passages. Romans 11 was true in the Acts period. Ephesians 3 is true now.

**Ephesians 3:7.** *I became a servant of this gospel by the gift of God's grace given me through the working of His power.*

Paul became a servant of this secret. Paul considers himself to be a servant, almost an errand-boy, of the secret that he is now setting forth. This position does not bother him, for this is according to the gift of God's grace given to him through the working of His power. God's power had made Paul a servant in this great work.

I wonder if we ever consider what a great thing it is to truly be a servant of God? The position of a servant is considered a lowly one, but the glory of a servant is in the greatness of his master. To be the servant of a great lord is a much more honourable position than to be the servant of some lowborn noble. So to be a servant of our great God and Saviour in something as crucial as the great secret of God's work today is a most honourable position indeed. Paul considered it a gift, given to him by God's power. Similarly, we should consider it an honour to serve God and His truth today, and be willing to put in maximum effort in seeking the truth, and proclaiming this secret of the administration of God's grace. Let us never forget what a valuable thing God's truth is.

**Ephesians 3:8.** *Although I am less than the least of all God's people, this grace was given me: to preach to the Gentiles the unsearchable riches of Christ,*

Paul does not specify why he considers himself "less than the least of all the saints" here, but it seems likely that it is for the same reason as that given in I Corinthians 15:9.

> For I am the least of the apostles and do not even deserve to be called an apostle, because I persecuted the church of God.

Paul considered himself the least of the apostles during the Acts period, not because he was less powerful than they were, but because he had persecuted the church of God before his encounter with Christ on the Damascus road. No doubt, that is why he considers himself less than the least of all the saints here as well.

As undeserving as he was, love and favour were shown to Paul, so that he became the one to preach among the nations the unsearchable riches of Christ. The word for "unsearchable" here is *anexichniastos*, and occurs only here and in Romans 11:33, where it is translated "beyond tracing out." The riches of Christ are unsearchable and untraceable. I believe this is talking about the riches of Christ that are given to us in the dispensation of grace. In Colossians 3:3, Paul declares, *"For you died, and your life is now hidden with Christ in God."* In the administration of grace, our lives are hidden. This was not the case in the Acts period. The fact that someone was a believer was obvious. For example, on the day of Pentecost, tongues as of fire marked out the believers (Acts 2:3). In the house of Cornelius, the gift of languages clearly demonstrated those who believed (Acts 10:46). Christ enumerated five signs that would follow those that believed (Mark 16:17-18). In the Acts period, those who believed and those who did not was not a hidden thing at all, but rather was open and plain to see. It is not so in our day. Unless we choose to proclaim it, no one can just know by simply looking at us that we have life in Christ. There is no open or obvious sign of it, and if someone tried to fake having life in Christ, it may be hard to tell the difference without getting to know the person well. That is because our lives are not openly demonstrated by miracles and plain to see. They are hidden with Christ in God.

Christ is just as hidden to the world today as we are. Many know of the man named Jesus Christ, but few are aware of exactly Who He is and what He is in the sight of God. The truth of Who Christ is as a whole is hidden from the world, but that is not the end of the story. Colossians 3:4 assures us that someday, things will change. *"When Christ, who is your life, appears, then you also will appear with him in glory."* Someday, Christ will no longer be hidden. He will be revealed to the world. The word "appear" here is the Greek word *phaneroo*, and means "to shine forth" or "to be manifested." When Christ is made plain to the world, then we also shall be made plain. The truth about believers today will finally be understood by all.

In the same way, the riches that Christ gives us today through His grace are unsearchable. Some are always calling upon God to manifest His blessings to them in an obvious way. They say this because they believe that this will bring God glory. Others merely ask God this because they tend to doubt, and they want God to manifest Himself so that they can see it and believe. Those who ask this always end up disappointed. God does not shower His blessings upon us in a way that can be clearly recognized. Instead, He hides them, making them unsearchable, so that if we do not believe the testimony of God's Word, we might not realize that they are even there.

This passage assures us that as believers we are greatly blessed and enriched by the gracious gifts Christ offers us. He is daily pouring His rich blessings of grace upon us. And yet we cannot search them out. Strange coincidences may happen to us, and we cannot say whether or not they were brought about by God or not. We narrowly escape some danger, and yet we cannot say if God rescued us or if we were just "lucky." We recover from some illness, and we cannot say whether or not God stepped in, or if the natural processes He created in our bodies simply won out over the disease. We can often clearly identify blessings, and yet there is no clear link back to God that we can see. We may believe that our blessings are from the Lord, but if we do, this is based upon our faith. It is not a conclusion arrived at after examining the physical evidence. We have no evidence that could ever stand in a court of law that even one of our blessings came from Christ. And yet Paul assures us that Christ does have riches for the believer of today, *though they are unsearchable.* It is when we appear with Christ that we will come to know all that God did for us behind the scenes in the administration of grace. Then, we will see and appreciate how blessed we really were!

**Ephesians 3:9.** *and to make plain to everyone the administration of this mystery, which for ages past was kept hidden in God, Who created all things.*

Paul was preaching among the nations the unsearchable riches of Christ and setting forth the revelation that would allow all to see what is the administration of this mystery. Again the word "mystery" here should be "secret." This means that he was to reveal to men God's secret administration.

Just as Ephesians 3:2 teaches us that God's current policy is to act always in grace, Ephesians 3:9 teaches us that God's policy now is to *act always in secret.* At the present time, God does not act openly, and He does not act manifestly. We can see multiple examples of Him acting openly during the book of Acts. Acts period believers, from the very beginning, were hearing God's voice, seeing visions of angels, and being directed in miraculous ways. Since God began His secret administration, however, all such evidential miracles have come to an end. As Sir Robert Anderson pointed out in his excellent book *The Silence of God*:

> "The Divine history of the favoured race for thousands of years teems with miracles by which God gave proof of His power with men, and yet we are confronted by the astounding fact that from the days of the apostles to the present hour the history of Christendom will be searched in vain for the record of a single, public event to compel belief that there is a God at all." (Sir Robert Anderson, *The Silence of God*, Kregel Publications, page 18.)

This is very true. Today, we have no evidence that will stand up in a court of law that proves God is working. The only reason we know He is there is because of our faith. When you think about it, this fits very well with an administration of grace, for the best grace is always in secret. Suppose, for example, I had some poor neighbours whom I knew did not have enough money for food, and their children were going to bed hungry. Suppose I determined to give a monetary gift to this family to help them make ends meet. This would seem a very gracious act on my part. Yet suppose I was to hire someone to roll a red carpet out before me as I walked next door to my neighbours' house, to hire a brass band to march before me playing majestic music, and to have a crier go before me proclaiming, "This man is about to give a generous gift to his poor neighbours! This man is about to give a generous gift to his poor neighbours!" Would it still seem that I was being so gracious? No! Now it would seem more that I was doing this for the attention and praise that I would get. The best and most sacrificial thing to do would be for me to sneak next door and put the money in their mailbox or shove it under their door. I would be giving them the same gift, but this way, I would be giving it in secret, and would never get any glory for it at all. This is the best way to do something gracious.

Yet this would not fit at all with God working in judgment. I can always shove money under my neighbour's door, but if they owe me money, I cannot sneak into their house and simply take it! I need to do this openly, and I may have to take the debt to some authority. Punishments and rewards can rightfully be done only in the open. However, grace can best be done in secret.

So it is with the grace of God for us today. While God acts totally in grace, He also acts totally in secret. All His blessings upon us are given anonymously, and they are not given to bring glory to the One giving them. Thus, His grace towards us today is secret. This is the only appropriate way for Him to dispense His blessings in a dispensation of grace. Moreover, what God requires of us is also fitting for the administration of grace. Since God never works openly or manifestly, but only in secret, we must receive salvation by grace through faith without seeing. Therefore, all who believe today qualify under the words of Christ in John 20:29:

> Then Jesus told him, "Because you have seen Me, you have believed; blessed are those who have not seen and yet have believed."

We have seen no evidence. We have not had any vision or revelation of Christ raised from the dead. We have observed nothing that could be classified as hard evidence that would convince us that the Bible is true. There is no way for us to believe based on indisputable evidence. When we believe, we believe without seeing. Christ's words in John 20:29 reveal to us that this fact means that we are most blessed. To be a believer in God's secret administration is an impressive thing indeed. We have qualified as those who believe without seeing.

Then, Paul reveals that this secret administration was hidden in God, Who created all things through Jesus Christ. We must take careful note of this, for some have imagined that they have found this secret hidden in obscure references in the earlier parts of Scripture. Yet this was hidden in God, not in the Bible. The truth of God working in a secret administration of grace was not revealed until God gave the revelation of it to Paul after Acts 28:28, and thus it must be contained solely in the last seven letters of Paul.

**Ephesians 3:10.** *His intent was that now, through the church, the manifold wisdom of God should be made known to the rulers and authorities in the heavenly realms,*

Now, Paul comes to the purpose for which God is doing all this. Why did God introduce this current work, never before revealed as part of His plan, into His purpose and program? Why has He chosen to bless all nations equally and jointly, rather than through Israel? Why has He begun a secret administration of grace?

In this verse, the Holy Spirit reveals that all this has been done to the intent that now the manifold wisdom of God is being made known through the church to the rulers and authorities in the heavenly realms. God's purpose now is to reveal Himself to those beings in the heavenly realms. His focus is not primarily men on earth, because God is working in silence and few here know or understand His manifold wisdom. Imagine how much more of God could be known if only He would work openly! Isaiah 26:9b-10 tells us the truth about this.

> When Your judgments come upon the earth, the people of the world learn righteousness. Though grace is shown to the wicked, they do not learn righteousness; even in a land of uprightness they go on doing evil and regard not the majesty of the LORD.

God knows that showing grace to the wicked will generally not teach them to change their ways and act righteously. On the other hand, He knows very well that when His judgments come upon the earth, people will learn about righteousness. The grace that God is showing today will never result in all people on earth coming to God. Yet the main focus of God's revelation right now is on the heavenly rulers and authorities. These are the ones who are to learn from what He is doing among us today.

Yet if we were to look at other passages, we will learn that, though great lessons might now be learned by heavenly beings, in the time to come, God's work among us today and the grace He is showing us will have an impact that goes far beyond this. In Ephesians 2:7, the Holy Spirit declares,

> in order that in the coming ages He might show the incomparable riches of His grace, expressed in His kindness to us in Christ Jesus.

The kindness God is showing us now in Christ Jesus will be used in all His purposes and future plans to show how incomparably rich His grace is. This was the reason God interrupted His past work with Israel. God has always had great plans for the nation of

Israel. He has made them promises He can never break, and that He will never break. One example is found in Jeremiah 31:35-36. Right after making the great promise of His new covenant with Israel, He makes this solemn statement about that people He chose long ago.

> This is what the LORD says,
> He who appoints the sun to shine by day,
> who decrees the moon and stars to shine by night,
> who stirs up the sea so that its waves roar—
> the LORD Almighty is his name:
> "Only if these decrees vanish from my sight,"
> declares the LORD,
> "will the descendants of Israel ever cease
> to be a nation before me."

God will never turn from the descendants of Israel completely. They will be a nation before Him forever. Yet today He has made a break from His purposes for them to work among all nations, and He has done this to display a great truth about His own character and grace. Some might balk at this, wondering whether God would really bring about a two thousand year break in His purposes for Israel and this earth to reveal a truth about Himself to the heavenly beings. Yet for one who is well versed in Scripture, this will be no surprise. God at other times and in other situations does things solely for His name's sake, or for His great name. Consider the example in Ezekiel 36:22.

> "Therefore say to the house of Israel, 'This is what the Sovereign LORD says: It is not for your sake, O house of Israel, that I am going to do these things, but for the sake of My holy name, which you have profaned among the nations where you have gone.'"

Since God in other situations acted to promote His holy name, we should not be surprised to find that His primary purpose in the work He is doing among us today is to likewise teach a truth about Himself. The truth of His grace is a marvellous truth, and in His work toward us today, He works to exalt it, first among the heavenly principalities and powers, and then among all His creatures in the ages to come. What a privilege it is for us to be an object lesson of His grace!

**Ephesians 3:11.** *according to His eternal purpose which He accomplished in Christ Jesus our Lord.*

Since we know that the great work that God is currently accomplishing was not revealed anywhere in Scripture before it was announced by Paul in his prison epistles, we might be inclined to imagine that this work is related to an entirely new purpose that is completely unconnected to the plans of God that had been revealed in the past. Paul now assures us that this is not so. The current work of God and His present intention are both related to the eternal purpose towards which God has always been working. Paul proclaims this purpose as already accomplished in Christ Jesus our Lord. Though we know that much of God's purpose is yet to be worked out, God considers it already accomplished in Christ Jesus. And an important part of that work is His current revelation of His kindness toward us, and our being raised and seated with Him (Ephesians 2:6-7). God is still working on the same plan He has always had (Ephesians 1:4), though we might be in a different and previously-unrevealed part of it.

**Ephesians 3:12.** *In Him and through faith in Him we may approach God with freedom and confidence.*

We are blessed to have permission to approach God because of our position in grace, which we receive by being IN Christ Jesus. The word "freedom" here has to do with openness, confidence, and boldness, particularly in speech. The word "confidence" has to do with reliance or trust. In Christ we can share our innermost thoughts openly with the Father, and have access to Him with confidence because of our faith in Christ. These are great privileges indeed!

**Ephesians 3:13.** *I ask you, therefore, not to be discouraged because of my sufferings for you, which are your glory.*

Paul, God's chosen vessel to put these great truths in writing, was currently going through much testing and many trials. Yet he appeals to his readers, based upon their free and confident access to God, not to lose heart at these things. Outwardly things might look bad, but before God they had every reason for complete confidence.

**Ephesians 3:14.** *For this reason I kneel before the Father,*

Paul, having finished the parenthesis of verses 2-13, returns to his original statement of verse 1, which had to do with his prayer for the believers to whom he was writing. He asks for them to have strength (v 16) and the indwelling of Christ (v 17), and goes on to ask that love would root and establish them (v 17), that they would be able to comprehend the love of Christ (v 18-19), and that they would be filled with God's fullness (v 19). These are high and lofty requests, and they show Paul's heart for those to whom he was writing. He wanted them to understand these truths so they could ultimately understand God and His love. What greater purpose could there be for the glorious revelation of God given in this chapter?

# In Conclusion

# In Conclusion

Thus we see that having a true understanding of the things Paul wrote about in Ephesians 3, and realizing what God's purposes for today are, is nothing short of a great blessing from God. Once we understand these things, no longer will we have to wonder why God is acting as He does, and why the world appears to be in such a mess. When God is acting only in grace, men who reject Him may take advantage of this to go to the limit in wickedness. When God acts only in secret, few will make the effort to fully get to know Him. Yet if we study to know these things, we will come to realize that God's purposes for today are great, and His purposes for the future are even greater. Thank God for the book of Ephesians, the book of God's present purpose, and for all the great plans He has that it reveals.

It is this author's conviction after studying this subject for many years that understanding truths such as the second great turning point in Scripture and the current administration of the grace of God is of the greatest possible aid in understanding the Bible. The reader of the New Testament who does not understand these things will always be trying to read the believer of today into the Acts period, or into the gospels, or even into the Old Testament, and so will always be puzzled by the obvious truth that things are different. When we read the Bible, if we wish to know and understand what God wants from His people today, we need to realise that God's current work began at the end of the book of Acts and we need to appreciate that Ephesians teaches us the truths about what He is currently doing.

To understand these two things can open up a new day with our Bibles, and help us to come into an ever greater knowledge of the truth. When we learn to leave the truths that applied to the time of the book of Acts in the Acts period, and to apply instead the great truths of Ephesians to ourselves today, then we will be obeying the command in 2 Timothy 2:15, and will be correctly handling, or rightly dividing, the word of truth. The author prays that the reader will grow in knowledge of the truth and of right division through these things as he has set them forth. May God bless us all in our studies of the Scriptures. Amen.

*****************************

# More on this subject

**Introducing the Books of the Bible**
**Brian Sherring**

The object of this well written book is to give a brief overview of what the 66 books of the Bible are about, and to place them in relationship to each other. As such it is a publication that many will find interesting and helpful.

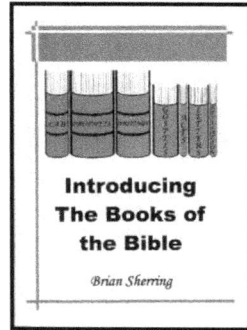

**Approaching the Bible**
**Michael Penny**

This book clearly explains how we need to Approach the Bible if we are to make sense of what God has said. It does so in an easy to read style and with an easy to understand method. Michael Penny does an excellent job of following the advice of Bishop Miles Coverdale, which was contained in the first Bible printed in English. That advice was based on asking such questions as:

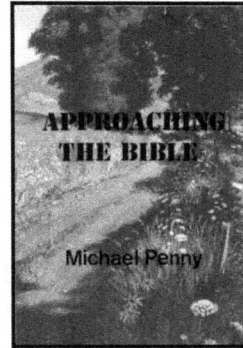

- "Who" were these words written to, or "Who" were they about?
- "Where" is this to take place?
- "When" was it written or "When" is it about?
- "What", precisely, is said?
- "Why" did God say it, do it, or will do it?

After asking such questions, we then will have a better understanding of the Bible and can "Apply" that passage to our lives today.

Further details of the books on these pages
can be seen on

**www.obt.org.uk**

The books are available from that website and from

The Open Bible Trust
Fordland Mount, Upper Basildon,
Reading, RG8 8LU, UK.

They are also available as eBooks
from Amazon and Apple

and as
KDP paperback from Amazon

# About the author

Nathan C. Johnson was born in Madison, Wisconsin in the USA in 1973. He attended the University of Minnesota, where he earned a Bachelor's degree in both Chemical Engineering and Chemistry. He also took enough Greek at the University to pass a two-year proficiency test. He currently works as a Chemist at 3M Company in St. Paul, Minnesota, USA.

He has a prison ministry and teaches at various churches and conferences in the USA. He has had articles published in *Search* magazine, but this is the first book he has written for the Open Bible Trust.

**For a full list of publications by the Open Bible Trust
please visit**

**www.obt.org.uk**

# About this Book

# The Jigsaw Bible:
## Putting the Pieces Together

For some Christians reading the Bible is like trying to do a jigsaw puzzle but without the picture. They find it hard to know which pieces fit together, and where they go. However, in his last letter Paul gave Timothy some advice:

> **Do your best to present yourself to God as one approved, a workman who does not need to be ashamed and who correctly handles the word of truth. (2 Timothy 2:15)**

The Greek word for "correctly handles," *orthotomeo*, occurs only here in the New Testament. It is a word that was common among tentmakers, which was Paul's trade. When making a tent, they would cut many pieces of cloth that had to fit together perfectly when the final tent was constructed. If these pieces of cloth were not cut correctly, they would not fit together, a bit like incorrectly fitting the pieces of a jigsaw together. It was crucially important that the tent-makers "rightly divided" the cloth. If they did not, they would not fit together to make a good tent.

This is the word that Paul used here for "correctly handling" the word of truth. If we fail to rightly divide the Bible, it will not fit together as it should. So the question arises, "How do we rightly divide the Word of truth?"

Publications of The Open Bible Trust must be in accordance with its evangelical, fundamental and dispensational basis. However, beyond this minimum, writers are free to express whatever beliefs they may have as their own understanding, provided that the aim in so doing is to further the object of The Open Bible Trust. A copy of the doctrinal basis is available on **www.obt.org.uk** or from:

**THE OPEN BIBLE TRUST**
**Fordland Mount, Upper Basildon,**
**Reading, RG8 8LU, UK.**

www.ingramcontent.com/pod-product-compliance
Lightning Source LLC
Chambersburg PA
CBHW060652030426
42337CB00017B/2584